CHAMPION of the Cornfield

Kathleen M. Muldoon

An Orphan Train Story

COVER-TO-COVER BOOKS Chapter 2

Perfection Learning®

Dedication

To Jody Cosson, Lupe Flores, Christine Kohler, and Carmen Richardson, my sisters in writing, with thanks for their love and support

Acknowledgement

Many thanks to Esther Espey Perryman, reading specialist and retired teacher from the San Antonio Independent School District, for her thoughtful review of this book.

Cover Train Image: Kansas State Historical Society
Designer: Emily J. Greazel
Illustrator: Greg Hargreaves
Cover Illustration: Greg Hargreaves, Mike Aspengren

Printed in the United States of America.
For information, contact
Perfection Learning® Corporation,
1000 North Second Avenue,
P.O. Box 500, Logan, Iowa 51546-0500.
Phone: 1-800-831-4190 • Fax: 1-800-543-2745
perfectionlearning.com

1 2 3 4 5 6 PP 08 07 06 05 04 03

Paperback ISBN 0-7891-5993-7

Cover Craft® ISBN 0-7569-1266-0

Table of Contents

Introduction

New York City in 1888

Tall buildings lined New York City streets in 1888. Most people living in the city were either very rich or very poor.

Poor people lived in crowded apartment buildings. Children often cared for themselves. Many of their parents were sick, in jail, or dead.

Some children without parents went to live in **orphanages**. Others lived on the streets. Those who got into trouble were sent to the New York Juvenile **Asylum**.

In 1854, a man named Charles Loring Brace wanted to help these poor children. He tried to find families to care for them. He started sending the children on trains to other states. The trains were called *orphan trains*. They ran from 1854 until 1929.

Posters were hung in towns telling people when orphan trains would arrive. Those interested in adopting these children met the trains. They picked the children they wanted. The children who were not adopted rode the train to the next town. Those not chosen at all went back to New York City.

People at the New York Juvenile Asylum liked Mr. Brace's idea. They started sending some of their children on orphan trains too. But these children were sent to people who could teach them a **trade**.

Most of the boys went to farms. Farmers signed papers agreeing to keep the children until they were 21 years old. The farmers agreed to provide them with food, clothes, and four months of schooling each year. They promised to teach the children to be farmers. These arrangements were called *indentures*.

Girls from the Asylum usually went to work as housekeepers or **governesses**. Their indentures ended when they turned 18.

Children were not allowed to leave the family or person who signed their indentures. Many worked hard. Some were abused. The lucky ones worked for kind people.

When indentures ended, they were given enough money to start new lives. By then, they were young adults.

By 1888, the New York Juvenile Asylum had sent more than 2500 children to Illinois on orphan trains. Most were indentured to farmers. They were boys ages 7 to 15 years.

Illinois in 1888

In 1818, Illinois became the 21st state in the country. The rich soil and flat land made the state perfect for farming. By 1888, over 3 million people of all **nationalities** lived there.

The main crops grown in Illinois in 1888 were soybeans and corn. Farmers also raised and sold hogs. Miles of railroad tracks lined the Illinois countryside. The trains provided farmers a means to sell their products all over the country.

The United States in 1888

Grover Cleveland was president in 1888. More than 60 million people lived in the United States. There were 38 states in the Union.

Some people had electricity. Some had telephones. Most traveled by horse, horse-drawn carriage, or train.

For entertainment, some people went to live shows. In the country, people enjoyed county fairs.

The sport of boxing was popular in 1888. New York had boxing **saloons** as early as 1841. But people who liked boxing had to sneak in to see the fights. Boxing matches were against the law in the United States until 1896.

Chapter 1

Fight!

"Fight! Fight!" Timothy Grady yelled.

I stopped punching Georgie long enough to frown at Timothy.

"Shut up!" I growled.

But it was too late. Boys of all ages formed a circle around us. Georgie started crying. I sat on his stomach.

"Fight! Fight!" the group chanted.

I looked at Georgie's face. A line of blood spilled out of his nose. I almost felt sorry for him. Then he opened his mouth.

"Your father's a jailbird," he whined. "And you're a stupid son of a jailbird."

That did it! So Papa was in jail. At least that's the last place I knew he'd gone. He might have died for all I knew. But was that Georgie's business?

My fists flew again. One hit Georgie's cheek. The other landed on his arm.

Then Georgie socked my eye. He kicked up his legs. His knees smashed into my back.

Suddenly, the shouting stopped. The crowd of boys stepped back. They made a path.

Mr. Salvatore Angelini walked through that path. He was head of the New York Juvenile Asylum. But he acted as if he were king of the world. We called him "King Sal." We called the asylum the "Castle."

"Tony Rizzo!" he barked.

He always spit when he said my name. I leaped off Georgie before King Sal pulled me off.

"Tomorrow morning, Rizzo," Mr. Angelini spat. "Do not report to breakfast. Report directly to my office."

I'd been at the asylum too long to be scared. The worst punishment was staying alone in a locked room. Sometimes that was a blessing! But missing breakfast was another thing.

I wanted to be a boxer. I wanted to be the boxing champion of the world. But I was skinny. The muscles in my arms were smaller than acorns.

I could not afford to miss a meal. Not even the yellow-gray eggs served at the Castle.

I stalked off to my cot in the **dormitory**. Already I felt hungry. I knew it would be a long night.

Chapter 2

The King's Offer

I was tired and hungry when I reached King Sal's office the next morning. I studied an old map on his wall while he read some papers. At last, he looked up.

"During the two years you have been here, you have been in trouble many times. How do you explain that, Rizzo?" Mr. Angelini asked.

Because your castle is boring, I thought. But I didn't say anything. I just **shrugged**.

King Sal looked at me as if I were a pesky fly. But there was so much he didn't understand.

I had gone to live with my grandmother when my mother died. After I had been caught stealing bread, my grandmother said she couldn't handle me anymore. So she brought me to the Castle in 1886. But she never wanted me anyway, and I only stole the bread because I was hungry. But why should King Sal care?

"What do you plan to do with your life, Rizzo?" Mr. Angelini asked.

"I want to be **heavyweight** champion of the world!" I answered.

The words flew from my mouth before I could stop them. But how could I? Boxing was all I dreamed about.

Before being put in the Castle, I'd seen lots of fights. My friend Benny's dad used to find out where the fights were. Then he would take us.

Once I saw the champion of Italy beat the champion of Ireland! The fight was in the basement of a factory on Fifth Avenue.

Mr. Angelini cleared his throat. "Fighting is hardly a gentleman's path to success, Rizzo. It is also against the law. It will never be allowed in America!"

I wanted to fight him right then. But he picked up a paper and waved it at me.

"I will make you an offer," he began. "A train is leaving tomorrow. It can take you to Illinois and your future. I want you on it."

My stomach flipped. Suddenly, I wanted to see what was on that paper.

Mr. Angelini continued. "People in Illinois are willing to take in fellows like you. You will live with them. They will feed and clothe you. They will teach you a trade."

"Why?" I asked.

"Because you need help and they need help," Mr. Angelini explained. "These are decent folks—farmers. If you accept my offer, you can become a farmer."

A farmer! I laughed inside. The champion of the world would not work on a farm.

I started to say no. But an idea popped into my head. Illinois sounded far away from the Castle. Maybe it was near the ocean! I could sail to Italy or to Ireland. I could begin my training as a boxer.

While I thought all this, King Sal explained the papers. But I didn't care what was on them. I had my own plans.

I shook hands with Mr. Angelini. "I accept your offer," I said.

"You won't be sorry," he called after me.

But I was already on my way to pack my few belongings. I could hardly wait to board that train.

Chapter 3

Where's the City?

That night, I dreamed that I rode a train with velvet seats. I dreamed that a waiter brought me dinner on a silver tray.

But the train I boarded the next morning was a nightmare. It was hot and crowded. It smelled like old socks and cigar smoke.

Seven girls and ten boys from the Castle rode the train. So did a bunch of kids from some orphanage.

King Sal sent Mr. Cooper with us. Coop was a good guy. He usually worked nights at the Castle.

But even he was cranky by the second day. We were tired of eating apples and sandwiches. And we were tired of sitting three to a seat meant for two.

I guess that's what made me throw my apple core at Timothy Grady. He was one of the few kids I knew on that train. Then I spit an apple seed at a girl's head.

Coop pulled me up by my shoulder. He pushed me down the train aisle and shoved me into an empty seat.

"You will sit with me, Rizzo," he said. "Maybe you can behave for one more day. We'll be in Illinois tomorrow."

At least I sat by a window. We passed nothing but trees. I kept watching for buildings. I kept looking for some sign of people. Where were the cities?

I began to panic. Would I be stuck in the middle of some wilderness? Would wild animals and snakes surround me if I tried to run away?

Coop was busy handing out sandwiches, so I couldn't ask him. Just then I spied Jeremy West coming down the aisle from the bathroom.

"Jeremy!" I whispered. "Sit with me for a minute."

He looked surprised. Normally I had nothing to do with him. But Jeremy was one of the few boys at the Castle who liked school.

He sat on the edge of Coop's seat.

"How close is the ocean to Illinois?" I asked.

He looked at me like I was from Mars. "The only big water near Illinois is Lake Michigan."

I thought a minute. "Does that lake go into an ocean?"

Jeremy shook his head. "No! Besides, the part of Illinois where we're going is surrounded by land."

I turned to the window.

"Take your stupid brain back to your seat," I growled.

I felt bad for being nasty. But right then, it felt like my whole world was falling apart.

After it turned dark, Coop plopped down beside me.

"Try to sleep, Rizzo," he said. "We should be in Greenville by lunchtime tomorrow."

I started to ask Coop if what Jeremy said was right. But he was already asleep.

I stayed awake. I watched the darkness outside. I kept hoping to see some lights, but I didn't see anything.

Chapter 4

Dullsville

"We're in Greenville," Coop called out late the next morning. "Grab your suitcases and line up in front of me."

The children from the orphanage had gone with families in towns we had stopped in along the way. Only those of us from the Castle remained.

We came out of the train onto a rickety **platform**. The train station looked a hundred years old.

Jim Kinlaw came up beside me. He was short and skinny. He had only been at the Castle for a few weeks.

"They shouldn't call this place Greenville," he said. "They should call it Dullsville."

I decided I liked Jim Kinlaw.

Coop led us down a dusty path into a building with long benches. "This is the **courthouse**," he explained.

"It looks like an **outhouse**," Jim whispered.

Tired-looking people sat on the benches. Some leaned against the walls.

Coop had the girls go with a woman to one corner of the room. Then he lined up the boys against a wall.

Some of the men came up. They looked alike with their rough, red skin.

"They're wrinkled as raisins," I said.

"That's how we'll look by the time we're 21," Jim answered.

I laughed. "I won't be here when I'm that old!"

Jim looked at me strangely. "Don't you understand? We're practically being sold. We have to stay with whoever picks us."

No, you don't understand, I thought. I decided to invite Jim to run with me. He was too skinny to be a boxer. Maybe he could be my assistant. I pictured us sneaking aboard a huge steamship headed for Italy.

A tall man pinched my arm. His face looked hard as a walnut. He studied me from the top of my head to the bottom of my shoes.

"You'll do," he said in a gruff voice.

Before I knew it, I was sitting on a bench while Coop and the man signed some papers.

"This is Wilbur Schultz, Tony," Coop said. "Learn all you can from him. Good luck to you."

The walnut man took my suitcase and nodded for me to follow him outside.

I should have run then. But two things stopped me. The first was that Mr. Schultz was bigger than the boxing champion I'd seen. The second thing was where would I go in Dullsville?

I jumped into the hay wagon. Mr. Schultz clicked at the horse, and away we went. Every so often, he said something softly to the horse. He said nothing to me.

The wagon and I bounced up and down on a dirt road that seemed to lead nowhere.

Chapter 5

Welcome to the Funny Farm

The house we stopped at was not much bigger than the train station. It sat in the middle of dirt fields.

Mr. Schultz led me inside. People sitting around a table stared at me.

"This is Tony," Mr. Schultz said.

He nodded toward a white-haired man who looked like he was asleep. "That's my father. We call him **Opa**."

Opa opened one eye and grinned. "Welcome to the funny farm," he said.

Mr. Schultz pointed to the woman next to Opa. She had rat-colored hair and a pinched face.

"That's my wife, Libby," Mr. Schultz said. "Beside her is my daughter, Gerta."

Mrs. Schultz peeked at me through tired eyes. Gerta made a terrible face. She tossed her thick yellow braids.

"Bony Tony, covered with hay," she sang. "You look like a scarecrow. Are you scared, Bony Tony?"

"Hush," Mr. Schultz ordered.

She closed her mouth but kept her ugly face. I brushed some hay from my pants as I glared at Gerta.

The other person at the table was a boy about my age. He wore glasses on the end of his nose, which was buried in a book.

"Franklin," said Mr. Schultz. "Show Tony where he will sleep."

Mr. Schultz handed me my suitcase. "You will share a room with my son. Supper is in one hour."

Franklin led me up a ladder to a small room. He nodded at a narrow bed.

"You'll sleep there," he said in a whiny voice. "Don't ever sit on my bed. Don't ever touch anything of mine."

He pointed to a bowl and pitcher on a shelf.

"That is my soap and water," he said. "Don't touch it."

I thought about punching him right then. But I had better things to do. I had to figure a way out of that crazy place.

I opened my suitcase. On top was a wrinkled picture of Paddy Ryan, a boxing champion from Ireland. I had watched him win a fight when he came to New York.

"Keep that dirty thing in your suitcase," Franklin said. "Do not put anything dirty in this room."

"What's your problem?" I demanded.

But he was already headed downstairs. I walked over to his bed. I brushed as much hay onto it as I could.

Then I stared out the small window between the two beds. I needed a map. I needed to know how to get to the water.

Supper was quiet compared to the Castle.

Mrs. Schultz put steaming plates of potatoes and ham on the table. Opa cut thick slices of bread and passed them around.

Gerta was the only one who talked during dinner. No one listened to her.

Franklin got up three times to wash his hands. He picked over his food like it was rotten. I was so hungry I felt like eating his too. But Opa made sure my plate stayed full. Once he winked at me. I decided I liked him.

I was just wondering what we would do until bedtime when Mr. Schultz spoke. “You may go to bed now, Tony. We get up at 4.”

I never thought I could fall asleep when it was still daylight. But I did. I dreamed I was boxing in the middle of the train station. I dreamed I knocked out Franklin Schultz.

Chapter 6

Chicken Droppings, Pig Slop, and Daisy Mae

The next weeks flew by on wings. It seemed as if my brain had left my body. My body became a farming machine.

Each morning before the sun rose, Mrs. Schultz woke Opa, Mr. Schultz, and me. She made us eggs, biscuits, and strong coffee. Then we went out in the cold.

My first job was in the chicken coop. The chickens squawked and pecked. They hated my cold hand reaching under them to steal their eggs.

I had to fill their dishes with oats and corn. I filled their pans with water.

But the worst thing was shoveling all those chicken droppings. I threw them out back into a huge heap of the stuff.

My next stop was the pig house. I hated those fat ugly animals! Even worse was their food. Opa called it *slop*.

I had to mix mashed corn, grain, and water. The finished mess looked like something the pigs had eaten and thrown back up.

After I poured it into their **troughs**, the pigs attacked it. They snorted and squealed. They gobbled it up as if it were a steak dinner.

By the time the sun was up, we were in the fields. It was the end of March. Patches of snow remained on the ground. But we still worked.

We mended fences that snowdrifts had knocked down. We raked last year's dead cornstalks. At the end of each day, we burned the pile we had raked.

Opa said that all this was to get ready for the big jobs. In one field, we would plant oats. In the others, we would plant corn.

I hated every job I did. My hands became rough and hard. Dirt got under my fingernails and stayed there. My back hurt. My head ached.

Daisy Mae was the only living thing on the farm that seemed to work as hard as I did. She was a gentle old horse. She was not sleek like the prancing horses that pulled fine carriages in New York. She sagged in the middle of her back. It looked like the whole world had sat on it. I knew just how she felt.

Every day, Daisy Mae hauled Mr. Schultz in the wagon. She dragged the **harrow**. She took Franklin and Gerta to school and Mrs. Shultz to town. She never seemed to complain. But I complained enough for us both.

Our workday ended at sundown. Then I had to face Gerta's teasing and Franklin's whining. I just ignored Gerta. It was harder to deal with Franklin.

All he cared about was my dirt. His weirdness about dirt made me glad for the dirt under my fingernails. One night, I dug some out with my knife. I flipped it onto Franklin's bed. He jumped up like he'd been burned. He ripped the quilt off his bed and raced to the ladder.

Stuff like that happened every night. I knew I had to make a plan. I knew I had to run away. But my body ruled. It would not let my brain think of a plan. It wanted sleep and made sure it got it.

Each morning when Mrs. Schultz woke me up, I groaned. Another night had passed. Another night wasted without a thought or dream in my head.

Would I ever get away from that farm?

Chapter 7

The Move

I know it sounds crazy, but I began to like the pigs. I think it was because of Champ, a piglet that the other pigs picked on.

It all began when a sow—that's a lady pig—had a **litter**. When the squirming pink babies fought for space under her to nurse, Champ always got kicked out.

I told Mr. Schultz about it. He put me in charge of that baby pig. I had to feed it from a bottle.

Don't get me wrong; I still thought the pigs were ugly. But Champ stood up for himself. He didn't care that he was ugly. And I know it sounds stupid, but I really think he liked me.

The chickens were another story. They still squawked and pecked and wished I would go away. But I began to feel comfortable in that stinky coop.

The weather grew warmer. My body didn't hurt as much by the end of the day.

Opa taught me to hitch the **dump rake** to the back of the wagon and Daisy Mae to the front. Together we raked up the dead cornstalks we had missed by hand.

I felt good sitting up there and letting the horse and rake do the work. Sometimes I even pretended I was in charge and owned the land.

One thing did not change. Franklin still hated me. He treated me like the dirt he hated.

One day, Opa, Mr. Shultz, and I planted oats all day. After supper, I crawled up the ladder and fell onto my mattress.

Franklin slammed down his book.

"Get outside and pour some water over yourself. You're dirtier than **swine**."

Before I knew it, I had knocked Franklin down. I had just landed my first punch when a hand gripped my shoulder.

"Get off him, Tony," Mr. Schultz said quietly. "Franklin, get downstairs."

After Franklin left, Mr. Schultz sat on his bed. My first thought was that he would send me back to New York. The strange thing was that I wasn't sure I wanted to go.

"Franklin's fear of dirt is a sickness," Mr. Schultz began. "It's a sickness in his mind. Now that it's warm out, you can move to the hayloft in the barn if you want. I will leave the choice to you."

I moved that night. The hay smelled sweet. Stars twinkled through the window above the loft.

Every morning after that, Mrs. Schultz did not have to wake me. Daisy Mae took over that job.

Before sunup, she began snorting and tapping her hooves in her stall. She neighed gently, as if she were saying "Get up, get up."

At night, I talked to her. I always saved her a carrot or apple from dinner. While she chomped it, I told her about New York and the Castle. I told her about my plans for becoming boxing champion of the world. But as I talked, I realized something. Without knowing when, I had decided to stay on the farm—at least for a while.

I think the reason had to do with my muscles. They were no longer the size of acorns. All that hard work was growing them. Now they were as big as apples!

I would use the farm for boxing training. My time and work seemed a small price to pay.

Chapter 8

Opa's Secret

We spent most of May starting the corn crop. Mr. Schultz got the soil ready. Poor old Daisy Mae pulled him and the harrow. It had big steel wheels that broke up the dirt as far as my eye could see.

Opa and I did all the other chores. I even helped him with the milk cows.

The worst chore was **butchering** some pigs. It didn't keep me from eating bacon and sausage every morning. Still, I didn't want to think about what would happen to Champ when he got big enough. I tried putting him on a diet. But he had other ideas.

On the first day of corn planting, even Gerta stayed home from school. She was supposed to help.

Opa tied bags of corn kernels to both sides of the wagon. It was hard to believe that these hard, dried up kernels would become new corn plants.

I drove Daisy Mae with one hand and dribbled kernels into the dirt hills with the other.

Gerta was supposed to drop corn kernels from the bag on her side of the wagon. Mostly, she threw them at me. The rest of the time she talked.

"How come you came here?"

"Don't you have parents?"

"Don't you care when kids in town call you names?"

"Papa says you'll be here for a long time. Will you?"

I was glad when Mrs. Schultz came across the field with a lunch basket. I was *thrilled* when she took Gerta back to the house with her.

Mr. Schultz fell asleep under the wagon. Opa stretched out next to me beneath a shady tree.

He winked at me. "Did you know Franklin's going away?"

I sat up straight. "Where?"

Opa smiled. "Going to live with his aunt in Philadelphia. Maybe he'll like living in a city."

That was even better news than getting away from Gerta.

"So, you think you'll like being a farmer?" Opa asked.

I looked at Opa. I figured I could trust him.

"Pretty soon, I'll be taking off," I said. "I need to start training. I'm going to be a boxer. Someday I'll be champion of the world. I need to leave soon. Maybe after the corn planting's done."

Opa looked at me strangely.

"Tony," he said slowly, "Don't you know? You must stay here until you're 21."

I laughed out loud. "I'd be too old to box by then!"

Opa shrugged. "That's what indenture is. My son agreed to take you in. He will send you to school four months a year. He will teach you how to farm. The indenture ends when you turn 21."

Opa leaned closer to me and whispered. "I'll tell you a secret. Wilbur plans to give you a piece of this land. Then you can start your own farm!"

Opa beamed like he'd just given me the biggest gift in the world. But I could not answer him. I felt angry, hurt, and trapped.

I wanted to run. Instead, I just sat there looking stupid.

Chapter 9

The Accident

Life was better without Franklin. It felt like an angry bee had finally stopped buzzing around everyone and flown away.

My mind stayed in a dark place. But my body stayed so busy that I could not figure out anything.

We finally planted the corn. When the green stalks peeked through the dirt I felt like their proud papa. I liked touching their leaves. They felt like silk.

One hot June day, Mr. Schultz took me off my job of plowing weeds in the cornfield.

"I need you and Opa to cut clover today," he said. "We need to start drying it to make hay. I'll do the plowing."

I missed sitting behind Daisy Mae on the plow. Still, I enjoyed swinging that big **sickle** to cut down the clover. I felt my muscles grow with every blow.

Opa sang in German while we worked. Time passed quickly. Soon Mrs. Schultz brought lunch. I had just chewed a hunk of bread when we heard an awful screech, then a thud and a scream.

"Wilbur!" Mrs. Schultz cried.

We raced to the cornfield. Daisy Mae was trying to scramble to her feet. The plow lay on its side. We could barely make out Mr. Schultz trapped beneath it.

"Help me get the plow off him!" Opa shouted.

Opa, Mrs. Shultz, and I pulled with all our might. Just when I thought my arms would pull loose from my shoulders, the plow flipped upright.

Daisy Mae was still harnessed to it. Quickly Opa and I got her loose. She limped off while we knelt over Mr. Shultz.

His face was the color of rain clouds. Blood covered his shoulder and neck. As Opa pulled away Mr. Shultz's shirt, we gasped. The blade from the plow had cut off his right arm just above the elbow.

Mrs. Schultz screamed. Opa looked like a ghost. I could taste the bread I'd just eaten getting ready to come back up.

Mr. Schultz moaned.

"We've got to stop the bleeding!" Opa said. He put his hand over the hole where Mr. Schultz's arm used to be.

"Libby," he ordered Mrs. Schultz. "Take Daisy Mae back to the house. Get Gerta to ride her into town for Doc Hanson. Then come back here with some towels and water."

I knew Opa could not hold back the blood much longer. Suddenly I thought about the tar we had used to repair the barn roof. Could that goopy stuff stop the bleeding?

"It's worth a try," Opa said. "But hurry! We're going to lose him!"

I ran faster than I had ever run in my life. I saw Gerta riding off toward town, her hair flying in the wind. I grabbed the pail of tar and raced back to the cornfield.

Mr. Schultz looked dead. Opa removed his hand long enough for me to slap the thick tar on the bloody stump. Then I held my breath. One minute passed, then another.

"I think it will hold!" I gasped.

When Mrs. Schultz came back, we took turns dipping towels into the water and wiping Mr. Schultz's face. He stayed unconscious most of the time. But once he looked up at me.

"Good job, son," he whispered.

Finally, Doc Hanson arrived. Opa and I helped load Mr. Schultz onto his wagon.

I started climbing onto it myself when I felt strange. Soon I saw the ground rushing up to meet me. The last thing I remember thinking was, "I'm going to faint."

Chapter 10

Daisy Mae's Fate

Besides losing his arm, Mr. Schultz had a broken leg. Doc Hansen said it would be months before he could work in the fields.

Everyone helped with chores, even Mrs. Schultz and Gerta. Each morning, we met by Mr. Schultz's bed. He gave us our instructions for the day.

"Make sure to get the hay baled."

"Opa, are the oats harvested?"

"Tony, you and Gerta get the best pigs to market. There's a sale on Saturday."

"I'm glad I can count on you, Tony."

And Mr. Schultz depended on me more and more. I felt proud, as if I were the best farmer in the world.

One thing that made our job harder was that Daisy Mae remained lame. Mr. Schultz advised us not to work her. That meant we had to do everything by hand.

One morning, Mr. Schultz called me to see him after lunch.

"I know you love Daisy Mae," he began. "But we can't afford to keep a lame horse. I want you to take her and a couple of pigs to market on Saturday. They might bring enough for us to buy a mule to help get the corn harvested."

I swallowed hard.

"I don't think I can do that," I said.

Mr. Schultz studied my face.

"You know we can't make pets of our farm animals. I have overlooked your attachment to the pig. But money we get from the corn crop helps us keep this farm."

Tears filled my eyes. I squeezed them back and waited until I could talk.

"What if we can get the corn picked without Daisy Mae or a mule?" I asked

Mr. Schultz shook his head. "That's impossible."

"I promise! We will!" I said without thinking.

"All right," Mr. Schultz said at last. "But if you can't, Daisy Mae must go. Her **fate** is in your hands."

We shook hands to seal the deal.

But that night in my loft, I wondered if I could keep my promise. I looked over at Daisy Mae. In the moonlight, I watched her rub her nose on the wood in the stall.

I knew I would work harder than ever to keep her. But would it be enough?

Chapter 11

We Are One

Opa and I practically lived in the cornfields. It was dark when we left in the morning and dark when we returned at night.

Gerta and Mrs. Schultz took over the pig, chicken, and cow chores.

By the beginning of October, the corn stood as tall as me. It was harvesttime.

Mrs. Schultz, Gerta, and I walked up and down the cornrows. We used gloves with pegs to rip open every husk to pick the corn. When the wagon was full, Opa hauled it to the barn and dumped the corn in a **crib**. Then he came back and helped us with another load.

At the end of October, Mr. Schultz came to help. He leaned the stump of his arm on a forked tree branch. He picked corn with his good arm.

"You've got the muscle of two men, Tony," he told me one day.

I'd been too busy to notice. Mr. Shultz was right! My arm muscles now looked bigger and stronger than any I'd seen on a boxer!

By the middle of November, we were halfway through. But acres of unpicked corn stretched as far as I could see. Even I had to admit that we needed a good workhorse.

One morning, I noticed how brown the corn had turned. I saw how tired we all looked. It was time to tell Mr. Schultz that I would take Daisy Mae to town.

Just then I heard a roar and saw a huge dust cloud. When it settled, a train of wagons and plows lined the field. Dozens of neighbors climbed down.

"Wilbur," one said to Mr. Schultz. "We've finished our fields. It's time we helped finish yours."

Opa put his hand on my shoulder.

"That's how farmers are," he whispered. "We are one. We help one another."

They returned every day. Boys who had made fun of me in town worked happily beside me.

At lunchtime, the women pulled baskets of food from the wagons. I made friends with fellows my age as we munched fried chicken legs and biscuits.

Finally, the day arrived when all the corn was picked. Neighbors piled some on their wagons to take to market. Others took some to shell. They brought back the kernels in bags for Mr. Schultz to use for feed and seed. They heaped the cobs in a bin for fuel in the winter.

"Nice crop," one farmer told Mr. Schultz. "I believe you'll be able to afford that nice **mare** I have for sale. Good for pulling that old plow of yours."

Mr. Schultz winked at me. "You've got a deal, Henry."

That night, I was not sleepy. I looked at the stars and let myself feel happy. Daisy Mae snorted in her sleep. I think she knew she was keeping her home.

Chapter 12

Champion of the Cornfield

Things were slower as it got closer to Thanksgiving. The weather turned cold. I moved from the loft into Franklin's old room. Mr. Schultz said I would go to school during the winter. So at night, I began reading some of Franklin's books.

Mr. Schultz returned to doing everything he had done before the accident. He could do with one arm what some men could not do with two.

One rainy morning after I slopped the pigs, Mr. Schultz invited me to sit with him in front of the fireplace. Gerta was at school. Opa had driven Mrs. Schultz into town.

"You have become a man, Tony," Mr. Schultz said. "I am proud of you. You are like my own son."

My heart beat so fast I thought it would burst.

Mr. Schultz stared into the fire. "I want you to stay with us," he said slowly. "But Opa tells me you have a dream. He said you want to be a boxer."

I gulped. I had forgotten all about telling Opa my secret.

"If you want to leave, I won't hold you back," Mr. Schultz said. "I can end your indenture. I can give you money to get you where you need to go. I owe you that."

I could not believe what I was hearing. Mr. Schultz was offering me a ticket to my dream. I also could not believe what I knew in my heart. I did not want to go.

I tried to smile so I wouldn't cry. "I'm kind of hooked on farming," I said in a croaky voice. "I guess maybe I'm happy just being champion of the cornfield."

Mr. Schultz laughed out loud.

"In my opinion, that's the best place to be champion," he said.

I reached over to shake hands, but Mr. Schultz stood and we hugged.

Then I ran out to the pasture to tell Daisy Mae that I, too, had a home.

Afterword

Most states did away with indentures by the early 1900s. But some states, including Illinois, allowed indentures up until 1927. The orphan trains stopped running in 1929. That also ended indentures for orphans.

Glossary

asylum	place of shelter for criminals or the poor
butcher	to kill and prepare the meat of an animal for food
courthouse	building where law cases are heard by a judge
crib	small building with slatted sides used for storing grain, especially corn
dormitory	large room in which many people sleep
dump rake	large piece of farm equipment that picks up sticks, stalks, and other debris, usually dragged through a field by a horse

fate	what will happen as a final outcome
governess	woman who cares for and teaches other people's children in their home
harrow	piece of farm equipment with sharp teeth or disks that is used to break up soil and clods of dirt and smooth the plowed field
heavyweight	in boxing, a top weight class for boxers who weigh more than 175 pounds
litter	group of young animals born at the same time from the same mother
mare	adult female horse
nationality	state of belonging to a specific nation

opa	German word for "grandfather"
orphanage	place that cares for children without parents, usually run by the local government or a charity
outhouse	outdoor toilet that is a small building that encloses a seat with a hole in it, usually built over a pit
platform	raised structure beside the track at a train station that makes it easier to get on and off a train
saloon	elaborately decorated public hall

shrug	to raise and drop the shoulders, especially to show indifference or lack of knowledge
sickle	sharp hand tool with a curved blade used to cut tall grass or grain
swine	pig, hog, or boar
trade	job or occupation
trough	long, low, narrow, open container that holds feed or water for animals

About the Author

Kathleen Muldoon is a staff writer for a local newspaper in San Antonio, Texas. In her free time, she likes to write for children. She is the author of a picture book, *Princess Pooh,* and her work has appeared in many children's magazines. She has also written other Cover-to-Cover books including *Island of Hope, Beyond the Mountains,* and *Join Hands and Sing.* She especially enjoys writing fiction and nonfiction involving animals and also loves to write original and retold folktales.

When not writing, Kathleen enjoys reading, visiting the many historical sites in Texas, collecting old postcards, and playing with her cat, Prissy.